Logo 5

An International Collection of Logo Design
Logogestaltung im internationalen Überblick
Une compilation internationale sur le design de logos

CEO & Creative Director: B. Martin Pedersen

Publisher: Doug Wolske
Publications Director: Michael Gerbino

Editors: Andrea Birnbaum, Heinke Jenssen
Associate Editor: Michael Porciello

Art Director: Lauren Slutsky
Design & Production Assistant: Joseph Liotta

Published by Graphis Inc.

(opposite and next pages: Logo for Shiel Sexton Construction Management created by Young & Laramore)

Contents Inhalt Sommaire

Remarks: We extend our heartfelt thanks to contributors throughout the world who have made it possible to publish a wide and international spectrum of the best work in this field. Entry instructions for all Graphis Books may be requested from: **Graphis Inc.**, 307 Fifth Avenue, Tenth Floor, New York, NY 10016, or at our Website, www.graphis.com. *Anmerkungen:* Unser Dank gilt den Einsendern aus aller Welt, die es uns ermöglicht haben, ein breites, internationales Spektrum der besten Arbeiten zu veröffentlichen. Teilnahmebe-dingungen für die Graphis-Bücher sind erhältlich bei: **Graphis Inc.**, 307 Fifth Avenue, Tenth Floor, New York, NY 10016, USA. Aktuelle Informationen finden Sie auch unter www.graphis.com. *Remerciements:* Nous remercions les participants du monde entier qui ont rendu possible la publication de cet ouvrage offrant un panorama complet des meilleurs travaux. Les modalités d'inscription peuvent être obtenues auprès de: **Graphis Inc.**, 307 Fifth Avenue, Tenth Floor, New York, NY 10016. Pour obtenir des informations actuelles, veuillez taper www.graphis.com. © Copyright under universal copy-right convention copyright © 2001 by Graphis Inc., 307 Fifth Avenue, Tenth Floor, New York, NY 10016. Jacket and book design copyright © 2001 by Graphis, Inc. No part of this book may be reproduced in any form without written permission of the publisher. ISBN: 1-888001-54-2 Printed in Korea.

1

2

3

4

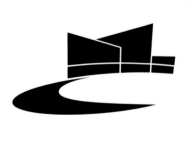

5

6

7

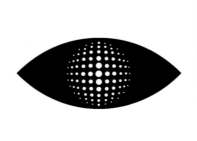

8

9

10

Of the exceptional work submitted for Graphis Logo 5, it was our job to extract only the best of the best. The collection you hold in your hands is just that, visual solutions for more than 400 identities hailing from all corners of the earth. Above and beyond recognizing these outstanding works, here we've selected what we deem the ten strongest, and have presented each with a brief statement by its designer explaining the strategy that was used. Graphis congratulates the designers and clients included in this volume, and is especially proud to feature its top ten selections:

1. Young & Laramore
Creative Director: Carolyn Hadlock
Art Director: Matt Ganser
Sculptor: David Bellamy
Photographer: Tod Martens
Client: Shiel Sexton
Comments
As a competitor in the crowded field of construction management, Shiel Sexton approached us with two major goals. First, architects had to be convinced that Shiel Sexton employed sensitive, insightful workers capable of sharing another's creative vision. Second, the company needed to communicate their dedication to thoroughly superior craftsmanship, or, as the company puts it, "building from the inside out."
We set out to design an identity by creating various sculptures, each focusing on a separate element of the construction process. After photographing the pieces for identity purposes, we installed them in Shiel Sexton's corporate headquarters. Clients, architects and employees alike enthusiastically embraced this distinctive identity system. And somewhere, devotees of the Western alphabet's 19th letter are making merry far into the night.

2. Alternativ Studio
Art Director and Designer: Péter Vajda
Photographer: András Láng-Miticzky
Client: Aedificium
Comments
Aedificum, dealing with design, construction and renovation since 1996, commissioned me to design their corporate logo using the "æ" ligature. The geometrical a and e letters used in the logo are the same characters, only they are turned around by 180 degree. I worked out the 3 dimensional end result by developing further the 2 dimensional version. The logo I designed in such a manner reminds the viewer of the construction of a building. Thus the æ ligature satisfies the request of the contractor, while at the same time suggesting the specific business the company is undertaking. This logo can also be realized in a three dimensional space in various sizes to fit the surroundings.

3. Chaney Nieman Munson & Son with Catapult Strategic Design
Art Director, Designer and Illustrator: Randy Heil
Client: Catapult Strategic Design

Comments
As a marketing communications and design firm that embraces a strategic, disciplined approach to client's brand development, Catapult Strategic Design sought to create a logo mark that would communicate its descriptive name and concept, to build brands and launch them forward in the marketplace.
To this end, we designed a mark that was simple, conceptual, and compelling. The message it conveyed clearly put Catapult in the industry in which it competes—marketing communications and design.

4. Felixsockwell.com
Art Director and Illustrator: Felix Sockwell
Client: Kaelson Landscaping
Comments
Kaelson Integrated Landscapes does business for both indoor and outdoor environments, so these two ficus leaves were a perfect choice. Unfortunately, the stem wouldn't act like a K, so I clipped one off a peach tree and pinned the two together during the photo shoot.
My client, Gary, was thrilled to have something that was grown in his atrium as the mark for his company. The results have been more than remarkable. He and his clients love the mark, and hearing the process by which it was created.

5. Brinkley Design
Designer: Leigh Brinkley
Photographer: Steve Little
Client: Stadium Food and Beverage
Comments
It's very simple. The owners of the Carolina Panthers NFL football team had recently purchased the entire food and beverage service at their home field, Ericsson Stadium, and named it Stadium Food and Beverage. The name alone composed 99% of the creative brief from the client. The other 1% was this statement, "Come up with something creative." We showed them one idea, without even sketching. Our presentation, "Here's your logo, a picture of this football with the chef's hat on top." Their response, "Great, go with it." Isn't it great when people let you do your job?

6. Point Zero
Creative Director and
Designer: Jim Guerard
Client: Landmark Development
Comments
Landmark, a real estate developer, wanted a mark that had a sense of architecture and geometry, but was also bold and graphic. The most timeless piece of architecture we could think of was the pyramid. This is one of those cases when the best solution was also the simplest. We modified the L, added a shadow to give it some drama and the rest is history. The client fell in love with the logo the moment they saw it. In fact, they were so crazy about it they wanted to keep it even after they changed their name.

7. Thinking Caps
Creative Directors: Julie Henson and Ann Morton
Designer: Rolando Gumler
Client: DWL/Mesa Arts Center
Comments
The challenge was to create a distinctive identity that characterized the premier arts and entertainment center in the heart of downtown Mesa, Arizona. We chose to embrace the building and landscape architecture of the center and create an icon that would be representative of its very unique features. The angular theater buildings are nested together and create an "M," and the curved arc leads you into the center of the project. The client, architect and landscape architect each believe this icon represents their vision of the Mesa Arts Center. We do too.

8. you are not alone advertising
Creative Directors: Thomas Neumann and Stefan Weder
Designer: Thomas Neumann
Client: Judith Haarmann Fashion
Comments
Judith Haarmann is a designer of high-class cashmere and avant-garde fashion in Hamburg. She needed a new logo for her label that would communicate the simplicity and strength of her fashion. You are not alone advertising devised a logo using the initials of Judith Haarmann in Japanese style to express the couture's clarity and dynamism. Judith Haarmann doesn't only use the logo for her correspondence and fashion labels. She also ordered a three-metre logo flag that now flies over her Hamburg store.

9. Kellum McClain Inc.
Creative Director: John Athorn
Designer: Ron Kellum
Client: Sensormatic
Anti-Theft Technology
Comments
Sensormatic is the world's leading developer and supplier of anti-theft and video surveillance systems. Athorn, Clark & Partners, their ad agency, had the task of positioning Sensormatic for increased importance in a changing retail environment. One of their recommendations was to replace a corporate identity they felt was "dated, and would not be representative of Sensormatic as it evolved." We were hired to fulfill that recommendation. The solution was based on the eye, which is symbolic of all facets of the company's service. Video surveillance, anti-theft tagging, cashier monitoring—it's all about watching and seeing. The dots suggesting a convex pupil were inspired by an actual product: a camera encased in a reflective, black plastic dome. This mark really got to the essence of the company's service, without inhibiting any new interpretations of that service.

10. Realm Communications
Art Director and Designer:
Steve McGuffie
Client: TLC Resort Group/Ocean Ridge Resort & Spa
Comments
Ocean Ridge is located in a popular travel destination on Vancouver Island. The objective was to create a logo that avoided many of the cliches that are common in the identities of resorts and hotels in this area. Images of starfish, seagulls and sand dollars are almost routinely used and the client wanted to see something that identified the resort in a more sophisticated manner. We did explore a few of the cliched looks, to eliminate possibilities and to reassure the client that this was the right approach.
Inspiration for the logo came from the fact that many beaches in this area have large, abandoned pilings that, at high tide, are semi-submerged and create interesting refractions and reflections. Several concepts were presented, and the client selected this logo immediately.

opposite: OUN International logo by Takenobu Igarashi Design

Olaf Leu, The Logo: A Profession of Identity

Even the best-written publication on trademarks—or, if you prefer, brand marks or logos—can't disguise the fact that this branch of graphic design is not in the best of shape. There are many reasons for this. For one thing, the great masters of the discipline—Paul Rand, Saul Bass, Herb Lubalin, William Golden, Peter Behrens, and also Anton Stankowski—are dead. These names already mean nothing to the current generation of students. Part of the blame lies with the historians of design who teach, or rather fail to teach, and are more interested in Monet and Manet than Stankowski and Glaser. The fact is that many students of visual communication believe they can live without the example of their antecedents, conjuring their ideas out of nothing. But we've seen it all before—in fact, we've seen better before. But the industry, which likes to think of itself as so fast-moving, is also forgetful—just as well for the many "me-too" designs, which are nothing but cheap copies of logos featured in books like the one you have before you.

This takes us to another reason for the demise of the art of logos. Nowadays, the first thing you see on walking into a graphic design studio are piles of books lying by the computer, all marked with slips of paper supposedly pointing the way to a solution. It's become one big process of collecting: creating variations on a variation on a variation, a process accelerated by the possibilities of the computer, where all designs lie ready for the taking. There are countless adaptations of William Golden's "eye" for CBS. In every town there's an optician boasting a "similar" logo. There are also countless logos gracing the façades of banks around the world, all derived from the first modern bank logo—the one designed by Chermayeff for Chase Manhattan. Every one of them is a variation on the safe-key or Fort Knox theme. The simple, geometric designs were the first to be taken, and once they had gone nothing new was created.

Joan Miro's "España" symbol unleashed a trend towards an independent discipline of signs and designs. Suddenly everyone felt like an artist, but the dashing, graceful quality that comes across in Miro's logo was the work of a genius. Now we have countless "artistic" logos with broad, racy brushstrokes leading us to believe in a whole new world of symbols. Master-painter Matisse's rough cutouts started a mania that resulted in every logo imaginable—all that mattered was that they bore some similarity to Matisse. Whether Miro or Matisse, their creations were driven into the ground by "the others." A similar fate awaited the "I love N.Y." heart, which was heartlessly transplanted into hundreds of cloned designs. A veritable heart attack!

Now we have a total logo war, fuelled by chips and machines that make it all too easy to churn out variation upon variation in full laser quality. The result is an embarrassing oversupply. Would you like it square, round, elliptical or triangular? We have decorations and ornamentation that would be the envy of a Viennese pâtissier. But few are powerful, noticeable or noteworthy enough to make a substantial impression on the public. Rows of letters—only varying by the case in which they're written—graced with flourishes our pâtissier would be proud of: the fastest way to a cheap solution. Today's practitioners of the "art of symbols" have few inhibitions. They wield their powers with little sense of responsibility, and a naïve decorative urge. The meteoric rise of the new stock markets, for example, and the explosion of financial communication for IT companies, is creating wild demand for formal identity and logos.

This identity is easy to come by. Too easy. We observe an effect similar to the one described by Philip Johnson in an interview: "It's not a good time for architects. We have nothing to hold on to. It used to be different. Just think of the golden era in Germany, with the Bauhaus and Expressionism. Now architects just bluff their way through: it's investors who lay down the law, and they're more interested in profit than beauty." For "architects" read "graphic designers," and for "investors" read "clients"—Johnson's description fits today's "logotects" to a tee.

The moral of this story is that you can't create a real identity using purely formal means and "me-too" methods. The resulting identity will be limp and unconvincing, and the company that commissioned it will soon fall back into the gray of mass-produced goods.

Designing a logo, whether it's abstract, painterly, illustrative or based on typographic forms, is a job for an experienced specialist who can simultaneously think in terms of the company, the company's goals and form. But what we have in reality is the absurd situation of agencies pitching for advertising accounts offering to create a logo almost as an afterthought, an extra service thrown in as if it were a mere by-product of the advertising campaign proper. It will take the corporate world years, if not decades, to rid itself of the countless "soft designs" that have emerged in recent times. Then we may be able to start thinking about a redesign. I only hope that by then the generation at the helm will know, and appreciate, its antecedents.

I hope that generation will have learned to make proper use of the means available, that they will use the computer as a tool and source of information, and books like this as a model of formal qualities.

For over 30 years Olaf Leu owned a design office in Frankfurt am Main, Germany. Since 1991 his concentration has been on corporate design consulting, mainly in the area of financial communication. He has been a professor at the Fachhochschule Mainz for over ten years, and now runs a seminar on C.I. Design. He has been a guest lecturer at workshops and seminars around the world, and he is Life Member of the Type Directors and the Art Directors Clubs of New York.

Olaf Leu: Die Marke, Das Bekenntnis zum Ich

Alle noch so gut editierten Publikationen über Trade Marks, Brand Marks oder einfach nur Logos genannt, können nicht über den Umstand hinwegtäuschen, dass es mit dieser Spezies des Graphic Designs nicht zum Besten bestellt ist. Das hat verschiedene Ursachen: Zum einen sind die grossen Männer, die diese Disziplin meisterlich beherrschten, gestorben – so Paul Rand, Saul Bass, Herb Lubalin oder gar William Golden, Peter Behrens und auch Anton Stankowski. Schon bei der heutigen Studentengeneration ist zu bemerken, dass sie diese Namen gar nicht mehr kennt. Das ist wohl auch ein Versäumnis der an den Schulen lehrenden – oder nicht lehrenden – Designhistoriker, die sich sowieso mehr für Monet und Manet interessieren als für Stankowski oder Glaser. Es ist einfach eine Tatsache, dass viele Studenten der visuellen Kommunikation glauben, ohne die Erkenntnisse der Altvorderen auskommen, quasi ihre Gedanken aus dem Nichts heraus schöpfen zu können. Dabei ist alles schon einmal – und in besserer Form – dagewesen. Aber die Branche, die sich als so schnell darstellt, ist vergesslich, und davon profitieren die vielen "me-too"-Lösungen, die nichts anderes sind als abgekupferte Versionen – eben aus diesen "Logo"-Büchern.

Und damit wären wir bei einer weiteren Ursache. Wer heute ein graphisches Studio besucht, entdeckt sehr schnell links oder rechts neben dem Computer einen Stapel von Büchern, die, alle mit Zetteln versehen, den Weg zur Lösung zeigen sollen. Ein gigantisches Collecting hat eingesetzt, und so entstehen die Variationen der Variationen der Variationen, zusätzlich noch angeheizt durch die Möglichkeiten des Computers, der alle Formen bereithält. Unzählig sind die Adaptationen von William Goldens "Auge" für CBS. In jeder Stadt wirbt ein Optiker mit einem "ähnlichen" Zeichen. Unzählig auch die Bankzeichen, die, ausgehend von Chermayeffs Zeichen für die Chase Manhattan Bank – dem ersten modernen Bankzeichen – die Fassaden der Banken in aller Welt schmücken. So ein wenig Trutzburg und Tresor sind sie alle. Und die einfachen, auf Geometrie fussenden Formen, waren sehr schnell vergeben; danach kam nichts Neues mehr.

Joan Miro mit seinem Zeichen für "Espana" löste einen Trend in Richtung einer ungebundenen Zeichen- und Formendisziplin aus. Jeder fühlte sich plötzlich als Künstler, aber was so schmissig, so leichtfüssig in Miros Marke daherkommt, ist das Produkt eines Genies. Unzählig sind jetzt die "Künstler"-Zeichen, die mit flottem, dickem Pinselstrich so etwas wie Aufbruch zu neuen Zeichenwelten vorgaukeln. Das Malergenie Matisse löste mit seinen groben Scherenschnitten eine Manie aus, die in allen möglichen Zeichen endete – es musste nur so ähnlich aussehen wie Matisse. Ob Miro oder Matisse, ihre Erfindungen wurden von denen "da draussen" plattgewalzt. Ähnlich erging es dem Herz von "I love N.Y."; es wurde gnadenlos und ohne Herz – aber beherzt – in hunderten von ähnlichen Lösungen eingesetzt. Eine herzige Welt?

Nein, es herrscht der totale Zeichenkrieg, angefeuert durch eine Maschinen- und Chip-Welt, die es scheinbar so leicht macht, die hundertste Variation der Variation per Drucker auszuspucken. Das Angebot wird dadurch riesig.

Wollen Sie es viereckig, rund, eliptisch, dreieckig? Ein Wiener Zuckerbäcker hätte seine helle Freude an dieser Dekorationslust. Dabei gibt es nur wenige Zeichen, die sich kraftvoll, merkbar und merk-würdig in das Gedächtnis der umworbenen Öffentlichkeit eingeprägt haben. Die Aneinanderreihung von Buchstaben – einzige Variation ist die Gross – und Kleinschreibung – versehen mit der Dekorationslust des eben erwähnten Wiener Zuckerbäckers, ist der schnelle Weg zu einer Scheinlösung. Die Hemmschwelle ist in diesen Tagen deutlich niedriger, zumal sich im "Zeichen-Metier" Kräfte betätigen, die alles andere als verantwortungsvoll, dafür aber mit dekorativer und naiver Lust an eine solche Aufgabe herangehen. Das sprunghafte Wachsen des Neuen Marktes zum Beispiel, die geradezu rasant zu nennende Vermehrung der "Financial Communication", der IT-Companies, schafft eine Nachfrage nach formaler Identität, nach Zeichen.

Und diese wird schnell beschafft. Zu schnell. Hier tritt dann wie in der Architektur der Effekt ein, den Stararchitekt Philip Johnson in einem Interview wie folgt beschreibt: "Für Architekten haben wir jetzt eine schwache Periode. Wir haben nichts, an das wir uns halten können. Das war einmal anders. Denken Sie an die grosse Zeit in Deutschland, an das Bauhaus, den Expressionismus. Heute mogeln sich die Architekten so durch, es gibt ja genug Vorgaben der Investoren. Denen geht es in erster Linie um Profite, kaum um Schönheit." Man ersetze den hier verwendeten Begriff "Architekten" mit "Graphic Designer" und die zitierten Investoren mit "Klienten". Die Beschreibung passt dann haargenau auf die heutigen "Zeichen - Macher".

Fazit aus dieser Geschichte: Eine wirkliche Identity ist nur auf formaler Basis und mit me-too-Mitteln kaum zu erreichen. Die Lösungen wirken saft- und kraftlos, und die auftraggebende Firma gerät sehr schnell in das Umfeld "der Dutzendware".

Der Entwurf eines Zeichens – egal, ob abstrakt, malerisch, illustrativ oder auf der Basis typographischer Zeichen–braucht/bräuchte den erfahreren Könner. Die Person, die gleichzeitig in Unternehmen, Unternehmenszielen und Form denken kann. Agentur-Pitches um einen Werbe-Etat, verbunden mit dem Kundenwunsch nach einem möglichen neuen Zeichen, sind abstrus, wenn dabei das Zeichen als fast unentgeltlicher "Mehrwert", als zufälliges Abfallprodukt werblicher Überlegungen behandelt wird. Die Unternehmen werden noch Jahre, Jahrzehnte benötigen, um all diese in jüngster Zeit entstandenen "soft designs" zu beseitigen. Man spricht dann von einem Redesign. Es ist zu hoffen, dass dann eine Generation am Ruder ist, die Vorbilder, die der Altvorderen, kennt.

Es ist zu hoffen, dass sie gelernt haben wird, mit den zur Verfügung stehenden Mitteln, dem Computer als Werkzeug und als Informationsquelle und Büchern wie diesem (als Massstab für formale Qualitäten) umzugehen.

Olaf Leu besass über 30 Jahre lang eine Designfirma in Frankfurt am Main. Seit 1991 ist er vor allem im Corporate Design Consulting tätig, mit Schwergewicht auf Finanzkommunikation. An der Fachhochschule Mainz hat er über zehn Jahre lang unterrichtet, heute leitet er dort das Corporate-Design-Seminar. Er war Gastprofessor bei Vorträgen und Seminaren in aller Welt und ist Life Member des Type Directors Club und Art Directors Club, New York.

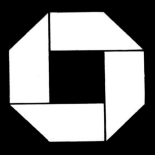

Le logo: la révélation d'une identité par Olaf Leu

Même les publications les mieux rédigées soient-elles sur les marques commerciales – ou, si vous préférez, les marques déposées, les logos – ne peuvent dissimuler le fait que cette catégorie de design graphique est mal en point. Il y a plusieurs raisons à cela. Premièrement, les grands maîtres tels que Paul Rand, Saul Bass, Herb Lubalin, William Golden, Peter Behrens, ou encore Anton Stankowski ont disparu. Ces noms n'évoquent déjà plus rien aux étudiants d'aujourd'hui. La faute en revient sans doute en partie aux historiens du design, qui enseignent – ou justement ne le font pas – dans nos écoles, plus intéressés par Monet et Manet que par Stankowski ou Glaser. Ainsi, de nombreux étudiants en communication visuelle croient-ils pouvoir se passer de l'exemple de leurs précurseurs, faire jaillir leurs idées du néant. Le résultat: du déjà-vu, en moins bien d'ailleurs. Le secteur, qui croit avancer à pas de géants, a cependant la mémoire courte, notamment à l'égard des créations «à la manière de», qui s'avèrent n'être que de pâles copies des logos tels que ceux contenus dans cet ouvrage.

Nous en arrivons ainsi à la deuxième raison du déclin des logos. Dans les studios de design graphique on voit toujours, autour de l'ordinateur, des piles de livres éparses, remplies de marque-pages indiquant des pistes de solutions. Collectionner est désormais un réflexe généralisé. Il s'agit de créer des variations sur des variations à partir de variations, et l'ordinateur, qui permet de tout copier et reproduire, n'a fait qu'accélérer le processus. Ainsi, on ne compte plus les adaptations de l'«œil» de William Golden pour CBS. Dans chaque ville, un logo similaire a été «récupéré» par un opticien. De même, toutes les banques du monde arborent sur leurs façades des logos dérivés de l'idée originale de Chermayeff pour la Chase Manhattan Bank. Tous sont des variations sur le thème de la clé de coffre-fort ou du trésor. Les formes simples, géométriques, ont été utilisées en premier et rien de nouveau n'a plus été inventé par la suite.

Le symbole «Espana» imaginé par Joan Miro a lancé la tendance de l'usage libre des signes et des formes. Soudain, tout le monde s'est senti l'âme d'un artiste, sans remarquer que le panache et la grâce du logo de Miro étaient l'œuvre d'un génie. On ne compte plus les logos «artistiques», réalisés à grands coups de pinceau et faisant croire à l'avènement d'un nouveau paysage de symboles. Les guaches découpées de Matisse ont lancé une véritable mode des logos ayant pour seule vocation de ressembler à ceux du grand peintre. Son œuvre, comme celle de Miro, a été nivelée par les plagiats. Le cœur du fameux «I love N.Y.» a connu le même sort. A voir les multiples déformations imposées au modèle original, on aurait presque un infarctus!

On assiste à une véritable surenchère, attisée par les puces et les machines: rien de plus facile, en effet, que de reproduire des logos déjà vus 1000 fois en qualité laser. La pléthore est inévitable. Carrés, ronds, elliptiques ou triangulaires? Il n'y a qu'à demander. Toutes les décorations et les ornements dignes d'un pâtissier viennois sont disponibles. Mais bien peu de ces logos sont suffisamment puissants, visibles ou remarquables pour toucher le public

qu'ils sont censés conquérir. Une succession de lettres – tantôt en majuscules, tantôt en minuscules – ornées de fioritures: voilà le moyen le plus rapide d'arriver à une solution pour le moins ordinaire. De nos jours, ceux qui manient le «langage des symboles» n'ont guère de complexes. Ils sévissent sans montrer un grand sens des responsabilités, animés par contre d'un besoin compulsif d' «en rajouter». La croissance fulgurante des nouveaux marchés financiers, par exemple, et l'explosion de la communication financière et des compagnies informatiques crée une formidable demande d'identité visuelle et de logos.

Cette identité est facile à obtenir. Trop facile même. L'effet observé est similaire à celui décrit par le grand architecte Philip Johnson dans un entretien: «Ce n'est pas une bonne période pour les architectes. Nous n'avons rien à quoi nous raccrocher. Il n'en a pas toujours été ainsi: il suffit de penser à l'Allemagne, à l'époque du Bauhaus et de l'Expressionnisme. Aujourd'hui, les architectes essaient tant bien que mal de tirer leur épingle du jeu. Ce sont les investisseurs qui font la loi, et ils se préoccupent davantage de profit que d'esthétisme.» En remplaçant «architectes» par «designers graphiques» et «investisseurs» par «clients» on constate que la description de Johnson s'applique parfaitement aux «logotectes» d'aujourd'hui.

La conclusion de cette histoire est que l'on ne peut créer une véritable identité avec des moyens purement formels et «à la manière de». Le résultat serait alors fade et peu convaincant et condamnerait à se fondre dans la grise uniformité de la production de masse.

La conception d'un logo – abstrait, pittoresque, illustratif ou à base de signes typographiques est – ou devrait être – l'affaire de spécialistes expérimentés. De personnes capables de penser simultanément en termes d'entreprise, de buts entrepreneuriaux et de formes graphiques. Mais nous sommes actuellement dans la situation absurde où les agences, prêtes à tout pour décrocher un contrat, proposent à leurs clients de leur créer un logo, quasiment en plus, gratuitement, comme un à-côté de la campagne publicitaire proprement dite. Il faudra des années, sinon des décennies au monde des entreprises pour se débarrasser des innombrables «soft designs» qui ont pullulé ces derniers temps. Alors seulement, il sera possible de repenser le design. Il faut espérer qu'une génération connaissant et appréciant ses prédécesseurs reprendra le flambeau.

Puisse cette génération savoir se servir convenablement des instruments disponibles. Puisse-t-elle utiliser l'ordinateur comme un outil et une source d'information et des ouvrages tels que celui-là comme un modèle de référence.

Olaf Leu a détenu une agence de graphisme durant plus de 30 ans, à Francfort-sur-le-Main. Depuis 1991, il travaille surtout comme conseiller en corporate design, notamment dans le secteur de la communication financière. Il a enseigné pendant plus de dix ans à la Haute école spécialisée de Mayence, où il dirige aujourd'hui le séminaire de corporate design. Il a été enseignant invité à des conférences et des séminaires, dans le monde entier. Il est membre à vie du Type Directors Club et de l'Art Directors Club, à New York.

(previous, from top) (1) William Golden for CBS/Columbia Broadcasting System (2) Paul Rand for NEXT, USA (3) Paul Rand for Westinghouse, USA (4) Rob Janoff for Apple Computer (5) Chase Manhattan Bank logo by Tom Geismar of Chermayeff & Geismar Inc.

BRAINSELLS

Design Firm **Stiehl/Otte GmbH Werbeagentur GWA** Creative Director **Reinhard Stiehl** Art Director, Designer and Illustrator **Robert Heuer** Client **VICO Werbe GmbH**

Advertising 16,17

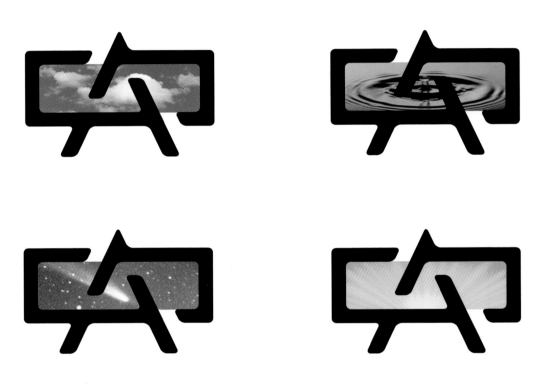

(this page) Design Firm **Planet Propaganda** Creative and Art Director **Kevin Wade** Designer **Martha Graethinger** Client **Adams Outdoor Advertising** (opposite, from top) (**1**) Design Firm **Wink** Creative Directors **Richard Boynton** and **Scott Thares** Designer and Illustrator **Richard Boynton** Client **Kruskopf Olson Advertising Agency** (**2**) Design Firm **Charles S. Anderson Design Co.** Art Director **Charles S. Anderson** Designer **Kyle Hames** Client **Sub Zero Advertising** (**3**) Design Firm **Webb Blevins Design** Creative Director **Larry Profancik** Art Director and Designer **Webb Blevins** Client **Advertising Federation of Louisville** (**4**) Design Firm **The Concept Farm** Creative Directors **Griffin Stenger** and **Gregg Wasiak** Art Directors **John Gellos, Gregg Wasiak** and **Griffin Stenger** Illustrator **Curtis Stenger** Client **The Concept Farm** (**5**) Design Firm **RBMM** Designer **Tom Nynas** Client **Lionsgate Communications**

(from top) (1) Design Firm **Bek** Creative Director, Art Director, Designer and Illustrator **Bülent Erkmen** Client **Ali Esad Göksel, Architect (2)** Design Firm **Pentagram Design** Art Director and Designer **Michael Gericke** Client **American Institute of Architects (3)** Design Firm **Classic Signs & Designs** Designer and Illustrator **Lillian Byrne Heyward** Client **Allison Ramsey Architects (4)** Design Firm **Catapult Strategic Design** Art Director **Brad Ghormley** Designer **Spencer Walters** Client **Dale Gardon Design (5)** Design Firm **Michael Schwab Studio** Art Director: **Richard Springwater** Designer and Illustrator **Michael Schwab** Client **Ferry Building Investors**

Design Firm **Classic Signs & Designs** Designer and Illustrator **Lilian Byrne Heyward** Client **Allison Ramsey Architects**

ibid.

(this page) Design Firm **Chermayeff & Geismar Inc.** Art Director **Ivan Chermayeff** Designer **Dirk Fütterer** Client **Dirk Fütterer** (2) Design Firm **Mother Limited** Creative Director **Mark Waives** Art Directors and Designers **Markus Bjurman, Cecilia Dufils** and **Kim Gehrig** Copywriter **Joe de Souza** Client **Britart.com** (3) Design Firm **Matthias Schäfer Design** Art Director, Designer and Illustrator **Matthias Schäfer** Design Art Director and Designer **Bob Wages** Client **Creative Club of Atlanta** (1) Design Firm **Wages Design** Art Director and Designer **Bob Wages** Client **Theben Art Gallery** (4) Design Firm **Liska and Associates Inc.** Art Director **Steve Liska** Designer **Holle Bode** Client **Reptile Artists Agent**

britart.com

(from top) (1) Design Firm **BBI Studio Inc.** Art Director and Designer **Zempaku Suzuki** Copywriter **Daisuke Shiraishi** Client **DOOV CO., LTD. (2)** Design Firm **Iconologic** Creative Director **Brad Copeland** Designers **Mike Weikert** and **Elise Woodward** Client **Sparkhorse (3)** Design Firm **The Team** Creative Director **Richard Ward** Designers **Richard Ward** and **Dana Winter** Client **Vemac (4)** Design Firm **Charles S. Anderson Design Co.** Art Director **Charles S. Anderson** Designer **Todd Piper-Hauswirth** Client **Isuzu Vehicross** **(5 and opposite)** Deesign Firm **Phoenix Design Works, Inc.** Creative and Art Director **Ross Sutherland** Designer and Illustrator **James M. Skiles** Client **Jaguar**

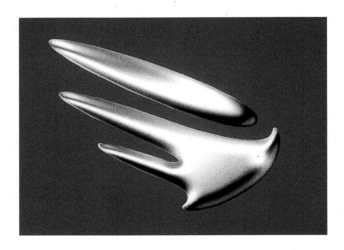

(from top) **(1)** Design Firm **Keith Harris Design** Creative Director, Art Director, Designer and Illustrator **Keith Harris** Client **Freunde der Antonow eV (2)** Design Firm **SDG/Scandinavian Design Group** Creative Director **Gary Swindell** Designers **Gary Swindell** Designers **Gary Swindell, Anne Marit Brenden** and **Benedicte Paulsen** Illustrator **Henning Arnesen** Client **Braathens (3)** Design Firm **Mires Design, Inc.** Creative and Art Director **José A. Serrano** Designer **Lucas Salvatierra** Client **Ocotillo Rocket Club** (opposite, from top) **(1)** Design Firm **Hirano Studio** Creative Director **Aoshi Kudo** Art Director and Designer **Keiko Hirano** Client **Shiseido Co., Ltd. (2)** Design Firm **Insight Design Communications** Creative Directors, Art Directors and Designers **Sherrie Holdeman** and **Tracy Holdeman** Client **Physique Enhancement (3)** Design Firm **Brand Group** Creative Director Art Director and Designer **Claudio Novaes** Client **Blondie Hair Design (4)** Design Firm **Felixsockwell.com** Designer and Illustrator **Felix Sockwell** Client **Salons in the Park (5)** Design Firm **The Benchmark Group** Creative Director **John Carpenter** Illustrator **Dick Sakahara** Client **Procter & Gamble, Olay Beauty Products**

Design Firm **Becker Design** Creative Director, Art Director and Designer **Neil Becker** Client **Latté La La**

Design Firm **Werkhaus Creative Comunications** Creative Director **Steve Barrett** Designer **Julie Poth** Client **Tully's Coffee**

(from top) (1) Design Firm **Sandstrom Design** Creative Director **Steve Sandstrom** Client **Radioland** (2) Design Firm **Liquid Design** Creative Director and Designer **Blair Kennedy** Client **Digitally Imported Radio** (3) Designer **Mark Ryden** Client **Radio Savant** (4) Design Firm **FutureBrand** Partner in Charge **Claude Salzberger** Creative Director **Michael Thibodeau** Design Director **Adrian Sanches** Client **PSN** (5) Design Firm **Sandstrom Design** Creative and Art Director **Steve Sandstrom** Copywriter **Steve Sandoz** Production **Sarah Cook** Client **KPAM Radio**

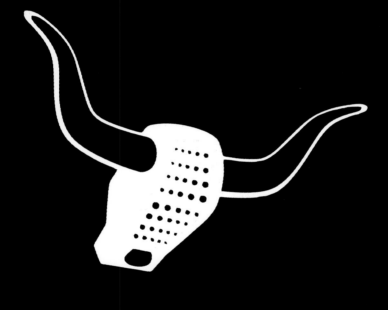

(this page) Design Firm **RAPP Collins Communications** Creative and Art Director **Bruce Edwards** Designer **Gus Granger** Client **Quantum Plus** (opposite, from top) **(1)** Design Firm **Hornall Anderson Design Works, Inc.** Art Director **Jack Anderson** Designers **Jack Anderson** and **Margaret Long** Client **McCaw (2)** Design Firm **Squires & Co.** Creative Director, Art Director, Designer and Illustrator **Paul Black** Client **Corban Communications (3)** Design Firm **Mires Design** Art Directors **José Serrano** and **Brian Fandetti** Designer and Illustrator **Miguel Perez** Client **The Yellow Pages (4)** Design Firm **Michael Osborne Design** Art Director **Michael Osborne** Designer **Michelle Regenbogen** Client **Asera (5)** Design Firm **Tom Fowler, Inc.** Creative Director, Designer and Illustrator **Thomas G. Fowler** Client **CPS Communications**

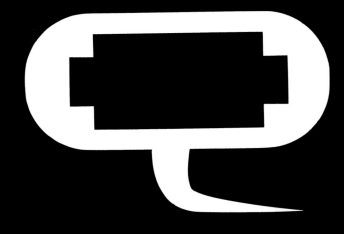

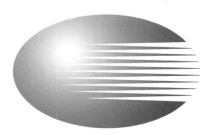

Design Firm **Landkamer Partners** Creative and Art Director **Mark Landkamer** Designers **Mark Landkamer** and **Gene Clark** Client **ILOG**

(this page) Design Firm **Sibley/Peteet Design** Art Director **Matt Heck** Designer and Illustrator **David Guillory** Client **Mother Hen Software** (opposite, from top) (**1**) Art Directors and Designers **Kristine Murphy** and **Brandon Murphy** Client **Black Rhino Graphics** (**2**) Creative Director and Designer **Brandon Murphy** Client **Brandon Murphy** Client **Mother Hen Software** (opposite, from top) (**1**) Art Directors and Designers **Kristine Murphy** and **Brandon Murphy** Client **Black Rhino Graphics** (**2**) Creative Director and Designer **Bob Dennard** Illustrator **James Lacey** Client **Maverick Technology** (**5**) Design Firm **Dennard, Lacey & Associates** Creative Director **Bob Dennard** Designer and Illustrator **Keith Carroll** Client **Coreintellect** David Suh** Client **Informix Corporation** (**4**) Design Firm **Dennard, Lacey & Associates** Creative Director and Designer **Bob Bob Dennard** Designer and Illustrator **David Guillory** Client **Mother Hen Software** (opposite, from top) (**1**) Art Directors and Designers **Kristine Murphy** and **Brandon Murphy** Client **Black Rhino Graphics** (**2**) Creative Director and Designer **Brandon Murphy** Client **Mother Hen Software**

TH+NK

(from top) (1) Design Firm **VSA Partners** Creative Directors **Curt Schreiber** and **Tom Raith** Designers **Susana Rodriguez De Tembleque, Hans Seeger** and **David Ritter** Photographers **Christian Witkin** and **Philip Lorcia Di Corcia** Copywriters **Fred Cuterl** and **Mike Wing** Client **IBM (2)** Design Firm **SGL Design** Creative Director **Art Lofgreen** Designer **Andrew Harrison** Client **Vizualize (3)** Design Firm **Woods & Woods** Art Director, Designer and Illustrator **Paul Woods** Client **Pocket Express (4)** Design Firm **AND** Creative Directors and Designers **Scott Arrowood** and **Douglas Dearden** Client **iArchives (5)** Design Firm **Kraus/Le Fevre Studios** Creative Director and Designer **Tracie Smith** Art Director **Roman Kraus** Client **Spectronic Unicam**

Design Firm **CKS/Partners** Art Director **Cynthia Occhipinti** Designer **Kevin Perera** Client **BackWeb**

(this page) Design Firm **Hixo Inc.** Art Director **Mike Hicks** Designer **Diana Gill** Client **Techworks** (opposite, from top) **(1)** Design Firm **Young & Rubicam/RPM Design** Creative Director **Sue Zeifman** Designer **Lenore Bartz** Client **Covad (2)** Design Firm **WangHutner Design, Inc.** Art Director **Maria Wang-Horn** Designer **Brian Jacobs** Client **Crossworlds (3)** Art Director and Designer **Joachim Schmeisser** Client **Unternehmensgruppe Witlenstein (4)** Design Firm **AND** Creative Directors **Scott Arrowood** and **Douglas Dearden** Designer **Scott Arrowood** Client **Thoughtstar (5)** Design Firm **Cawrse & Effect** Creative Director and Designer **Andrew Cawrse** Client **BB Interactive**

COVAD™

(from top) (1) Design Firm **Design Ahead** Creative Director **Angelika Feldhaus** Designer **Axel Voss** Client **CON Industries (2)** Design Firm **Squires & Company** Creative Director, Art Director, Designer and Illustrator **Paul Black** Client **Aquastar (3)** Design Firm **GSD&M** Client **Ranger Construction (4)** Design Firm **Hybrid Design** Art Director and Designer **Mark Ford** Client **Pierce Contracting (5)** Design Firm **Catapult Strategic Design** Creative Director, Art Director, Designer and Photographer **Peter Jones** Client **Ghormley Construction**

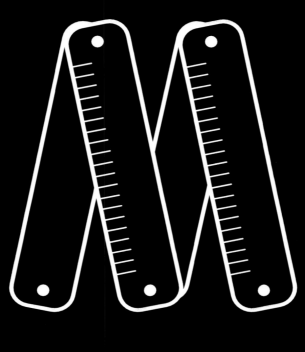

Design Firm **Prejean LoBue** Creative Director, Art Director, Designer and Illustrator **Gary LoBue, Jr.** Client **Linda and Manuel Herrera**

plural

(from top) **(1)** Design Firm **Lippincott & Margulies** Creative Director **Jerry Kuyper** Art Director and Designer **Brendan Murphy** Photographer **Andy Shen** Client **Plural (2)** Design Firm **Supon Design Group** Creative Director **Supon Phornirunlit** Art Director **Pum Mek-Aroonreung** Designer **Jennifer Higgins** Client **CJ Group, Inc. (3)** Design Firm **Y Design** Designer **Mayumi Shimisu** Client **Webrain (4)** Design Firm **Momentum Design** Client **Infopattern (5)** Design Firm **BlackBird Creative** Creative Director **Patrick Short** Designer **Emily C. Thwaite** Client **APEC China Business Solutions**

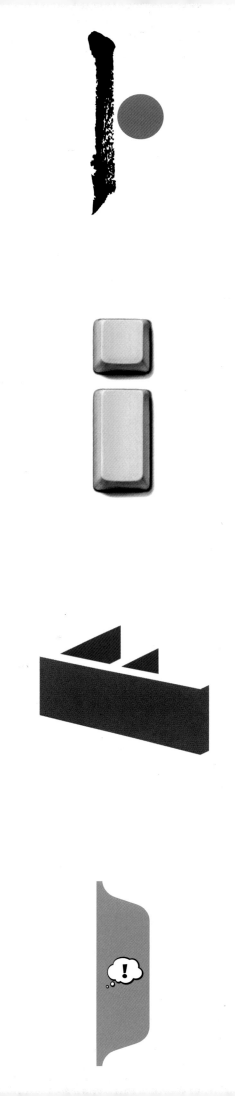

(from top) (1) Design Firm **Ron Kellum Inc.** Art Director and Designer **Ron Kellum** Client **Boiling Point** (2) Design Firm **Wink** Creative Directors **Richard Boynton** and **Scott Thayres** Designer and Illustrator **Richard Boynton** Client **Internet Returns** (3) Design Firm **Michael Courtney Design** Art Director **Michael Courtney** Designers **Michael Courtney, Dan Hoang, Heidi Favour** and **Brian O'Neill** Client **Fleischmann Office Interiors** (4) Design Firm **Hawse Design, Inc.** Creative Director **Robert Hawse** Designer **Brady Bone** Client **Composite Resources**

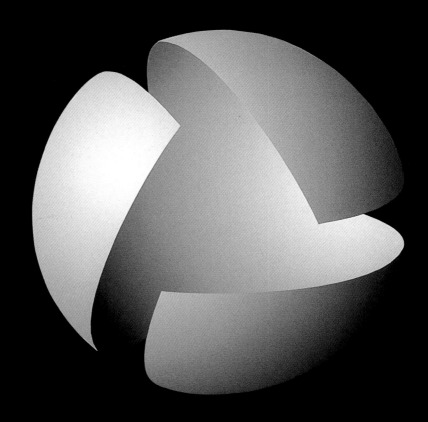

(this page) Design Firm **Planet 10 Studios** Creative Director and Designer **Michael Tuttle** Art Directors **Michael Tuttle** and **Jennifer Tuttle** Client **Netisun** (opposite, from top) (**1**) Design Firm **Carmichael Lynch** Creative Director **Michael Skjei** Designer **David Scrimpf** Client **Travelers Express (moneygram)** (**2**) Design Firm **Jager Di Paola Kemp** Art Director and Designer **Michael Jager** Client **Concept 2** (**3**) Design Firm **I.M.S.** Art Director and Designer **Jamie Anderson** Client **FinaTech Capital Group, Inc.** (**4**) Design Firm **Jeff Labbe Design Co.** Client **The Tech Factory** (**5**) Design Firm **Planet 10 Studios** Creative Director **Mike Tuttle** Designers **Mike Tuttle** and **Jennifer Tuttle** Client **Netisun**

THE TECH FACTORY

(this page) Design Firm **Curtis Design** Art Director **David Curtis** Designer **Chris Benitez** (opposite, from top) (**1**) Design Firm **Planet Propaganda** Creative Director **Kevin Wade** Designers **Kevin Wade** and **Martha Graettinger** Client **Merge Technologies** (**2**) Design Firm **Matthias Mencke** Creative Director and Designer **Matthias Mencke** Client **Matthias Mencke** (**3**) Design Firm **Sandstrom Design** Client **Epson America** (**4**) Design Firm **Supon Design Group** Creative Director **Supon Phornirunlit** Art Director **Pum Mek-Aroonreung** Designer **Michele Howley** Client **Advicezone.com** (**5**) Design Firm **A/3** Creative and Art Director **Adrian Pulfer** Designers **Scott Peramski** and **Adrian Pulfer** Client **Worthlin Worldwide Research & Pollsters**

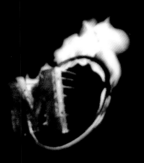

Design Firm **en Vision** Art Director **Howell Hsiao** Designers **Vladim Goretsky** and **Lai-Kit Chan** Client **en Vision Funding**   Corporate **64,65**

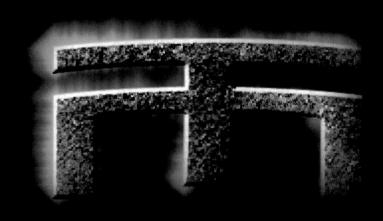

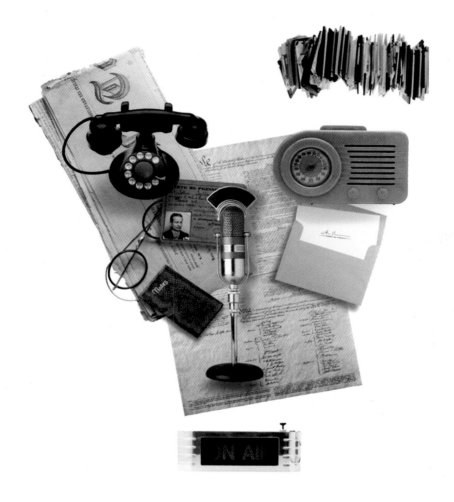

Design Firm **[code]** Creative Director **Lee Selsick** Illustrator and Designer **Paul Henriques** Client **Identity Public Relations** Creative Services **66,67**

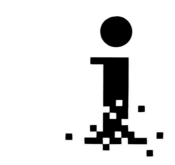

(from top) (1) Design Firm **Design One** Creative Director and Designer **David Guinn** Client **The Center for Craft, Creativity and Design** (2) Designer **Joseph Rattan** Client **Intelligent Control Corporation** (3) Design Firm **Mires Design** Art Director **Jose Serrano** Designer **Miguel Perez** Illustrators **Tracy Sabin** and **Miguel Perez** Client **The Express Group** (4) Design Firm **Robert Meyers Communication** Designer **Robert Meyers** Client **Robert Meyers** (5) Design Firm **Oakley Design Studios** Creative Director, Art Director, Designer and Photographer **Tim Oakley** Client **Spinning Gyro Graphics**

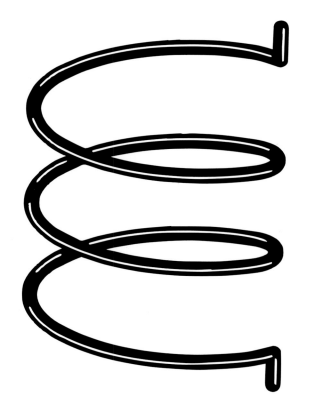

Design Firm **Smit Ghormley Lofgreen Design** Client **Comfort Coil Company** Creative Services 68,69

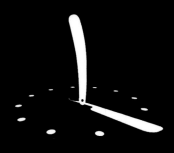

OO:O1:11

(from top) (1) Design Firm **Kirima Design Office** Art Director and Designer **Harumi Kirima** Client **Kirima Design Office** (2) Design Firm **Deep Design** Designer **P. Mark Steingruber** Client **Brenda Fuller, Business to Business Copywriter :3** Design Firm **The Corsi Group** Creative Director **Scott Springer** Art Director and Designer **Gregory Itts** Client **One-Eleven Recording Studio** (4) Designer **Rolando Muro** Client **5 o'clock barbershop** (5) Design Firm **Kirima Design Office** Art Director and Designer **Harumi Kirima** Client **Kirima Design Office**

Design Firm **Hixo, Inc.** Art Director and Designer **Mike Hicks** Client **Inkspots Production Co.**

Design Firm **The Benchmark Group** Creative Director **John Carpenter** Art Director **Jen O'Shea** Illustrator **Ken Meade** Client **Cincinnati Ballet**

San Francisco **Ballet**

Helgi Tomasson • Artistic Director

Design Firm **Frankfurt Balkind Partners** Creative Director **David Suh** Designer **Alfred Assin** Client **San Francisco Ballet**

POWERDESIGN

H A T C H

(this page) Design Firm **Gottschalk & Ash** Creative and Art Director **Stuart Ash** Designer **Sonia Chow** Client **Hatch** (opposite, from top) (**1**) Design Firm **Ambrosini Design** Creative Director **Ken Ambrosini** Designers **Anne Koenig Snider** and **Ken Ambrosini** Client **Ambrosini Design** Creative and Art Director **Ken Ambrosini** Client **Ambrosini Design** Designers **Anne Koenig Snider** and **Ken Ambrosini** Client **Ambrosini Design**
(**2**) Designer **John Fisk** (**3**) Design Firm **Laughlin/Constable (Griffin Design)** Creative Director **John Constable** Art Director **Mark Drewek** Designer and Illustrator **Jason Herkert** Client **Griffin Design** (**4**) Design Firm **Kirima Design Office** Art Director and Designer **Harumi Kirima**
Client **Kirima Design Office** (**5**) Design Firm **Wink** Creative Directors **Richard Boynton** and **Scott Thares** Designer **Richard Boynton** Client **Terminal**

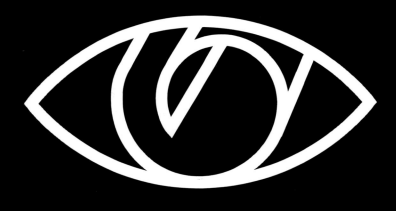

Design Firms **Chaney Nieman Munson & Son** with **Catapult Strategic Design** Art Director, Designer and Illustrator **Randy Heil** Client **Catapult Strategic Design** Design 80,81

(this page) Design Firm **Studio Dogan** Creative Director and Designer **Zrinka Penava** Client **Studio Dogan** (opposite, from top) (**1**) Design Firm **Supon Design Group** Creative and Art Director **Supon Phornirunlit** Designer **Scott Bouer** Client **Supon Design Group** (**2**) Design Firm **Art Force Studio** Art Director and Designer **Zsolt Kathi** Client **Royal Rocket** (**3**) Design Firm **Liquid Design** Creative Director and Designer **Blair Kennedy** Client **Liquid Design** (**4**) Design Firm **WPA Pinfold Ltd** Creative Director **James Littlewood** Designer **Paul Phillips** Illustrator **Nigel Burton** Client **Brand Alliance** (**5**) Design Firm **FDT Design** Creative Director and Designer **Katherine Hill** Client **FDT Design**

DEFINITION

DISCOVERY

DEVELOPMENT

DELIVERY

(this page) Design Firm **Thom & Dave Marketing Design** Creative Directors **Thom** and **Dave** Art Directors **Thom, Dave** and **Nelson** Designers **Dave** and **Nelson** Designers **Dave** and **Gins** Illustrator **Gins** Client **Thom & Dave Marketing Design**

Design Firm **Sandstrom Design** Creative and Art Director **Steve Sandstrom** Designer **John Bohls** Client **Fuse**

IRIDIUM

SALISBURY STUDIOS

ROMA

Design Firm **Hybrid Design** Art Director **John Swieter** Designer **Mark Ford** Client **Young Presidents' Organization**

Design Firm **Acorn Design Ltd.** Creative Director, Art Director and Designer **Frank Chan Wah Hung** Client **Parkview International Pre-school**

(this page) Design Firm **Packaging Create Inc.** Art Director and Designer **Akio Okumura** Client **Inter Medium Institute Graduate School** (opposite, from top) (**1**) Design Firm **Hall Kelley** Designer **Michael Hall** Client **University of Minnesota** (**2**) Design Firm **Catapult Strategic Design** Creative Director, Designer and Illustrator **Art Lofgreen** Client **Highland Hurricanes Elementary School** (**3**) Design Firm **Essex Two** Creative Directors **Joseph Michael Essex** and **Nancy Denny Essex** Art Director and Designer **Joseph Michael Essex** Client **aha! Process Incorporated** (**4**) Design Firm **Wink** Creative Directors **Richard Boynton** and **Scott Thares** Designer and Illustrator **Richard Boynton** Client **Eur-Am Center for International Education** (**5**) Design Firm **Arte Final Design E Publicidade, LDA** Art Director **António Antunes** Designers **António Antunes** and **Fernando Feiteiro** Client **Cinel Technological School**

(from top) (1) Design Firm **Gee & Chung Design** Art Director, Designer and Illustrator **Earl Gee** Client **Art Center College of Design Alumni Council** (2) Design Firm **Peterson & Co.** Creative Director, Art Director and Designer **Dorit Suffness** Client **University of Texas at Dallas** (3) Design Firm **Genovese Constenis Foster** Designer **Domenica Genovese** Client **Longwood College** (4) Design Firm **Project LoBue** Creative Director, Art Director, Designer and Illustrator **Kevin Prejean** Client **Assemblies of God Church** (5) Design Firm **Summation** Creative Directors **Bart Welch** and **Tim Fisher** Illustrator **Bart Welch** Client **Mountain Lakes DayCare**

TOKYO ENGINEERING UNIVERSITY

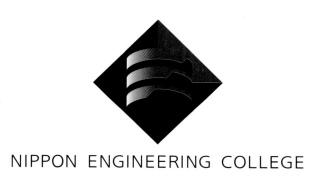

NIPPON ENGINEERING COLLEGE

NIPPON ENGINEERING COLLEGE

(this page) Design Firm **Graphics and Designing Inc.** Art Director **Takanori Aiba** Designer **Hiroki Ariyoshi** Client **Katayanagi Institute**

Design Firm **Margo Chase Design** Designer **Margo Chase** Client **First Light Dance Troupe**

STAR WARS
DEMOLITION

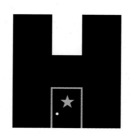

(this page) Design Firm **Packaging Create Inc.** Art Director and Designer **Akio Okumura** Client **X'l An Image (opposite,** from top) **(1)** Design Firm **Deep Design** Creative Director **Rick Grimsley** Designer and Illustrator **P. Mark Steingruber** Client **United Parcel Service (2)** Client **The Weller Institute (3)** Design Firm **Supon Design Group** Art Director and Designer **Brent Almond** Creative Director **Supon Phornirunlit** Illustrator **Jae Wee** Client **Cow Parade Worldwide (4)** Design Firm **Greteman Group** Creative Director **Sonia Greteman** Art Directors **Sonia Greteman** and **James Strange** Designer and Illustrator **James Strange** Client **Candlewood Suites (5)** Design Firm **Prejean LoBue** Creative Director, Art Director, Designer and Illustrator **Kevin Prejean** Client **Regional Aids Interfaith Network of Central Missouri**

Design Firm **Gill Fishman Associates, Inc.** Creative Director **Gill Fishman** Designer **Tammy Torrey** Photographer **Thomas Torrey** Client **Israel's 50th Birthday Celebration**

Design Firm **Viherjuuren Ilme Oy** Creative Director, Art Director and Illustrator **Ilmo Valtowen** Client **Siemens Finland Ltd. 100th Anniversary**

(this page) Design Firm **RBMM** Creative Director **Horacio Cobos** Designer **Rolando Murillo** Client **Freightliner** (opposite, from top) (**1**) Design Firm **GSD&M Advertising** Designer and Illustrator **Patrick Nolan** Client **Texas Aerospace/1997 Airshow** (**2**) Design Firm **Dennard Lacey & Associates** Creative Director, Art Director and Designer **Bob Dennard** Illustrator **James Lacey** Client **Dallas Symphony Orchestra League** (**3**) Design Firm **Hybrid** Creative Director **John Swieter** Designer **Ray Gallegos** Client **Dallas Heart Ball** (**4**) Design Firm **Tim Smith Communication Design** Creative Director and Designer **Tim Smith** Client **AIGA/Cincinnati** (**5**) Design Firm **Insight Design Communications** Creative Directors, Art Directors and Designers **Sherrie Holdeman** and **Tracy Holdeman** Client **Excel Food Company Awards & Recognition Event**

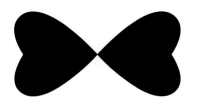

(from top) (1) Design Firm **Phoenix Design Works, Inc.** Creative Director, Art Director, Designer and Illustrator **James Skiles** Client **Walt Disney Company** (2) Design Firm **The Hot Shop Design Group** Art Director **Gloria Ailouny** Designer **Scott Markel** Client **Jeep Eagle Dealer Advertising Association** (3) Design Firm **Phoenix Design Works, Inc.** Creative Director **Ross Sutherland** Art Director **Grant Parrish** Designer and Illustrator **James Skiles** Client **Ogilvy & Mather** (4) Design Firm **Woodpile Studios, Inc.** Creative Director, Art Director, Designer and Illustrator **Peter Buttecali** Client **Wine & Spirits Wholesalers Association** (5) Design Firm **Phoenix Design Works, Inc.** Art Director, Designer and Illustrator **James Skiles** Creative Director **Frank Frasier** Client **Walt Disney Company**

(this page) Design Firm **A/3** Creative and Art Director **Adrian Pulfer** Designers **McRay Magleby** Illustrator **Dave Eliason** Client **Salt Lake Olympic Committee**

(this page) Design Firm **nick and paul** Creative Director **Nin Glaister** Designers **Amy Nadaskay** and **Danielle Stella** Client **Amy Coe Children's Bed Linens**

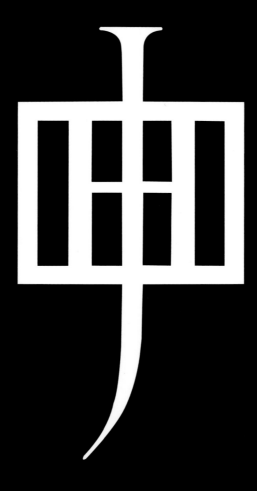

Design Firm **You Are Not Alone** Advertising Creative Directors **Thomas Neumann** and **Stefan Weder** Designer **Thomas Neumann** Client **Judith Haarkmann Fashion**

(this page) Design Firm **Sandstrom Design** Creative Director **Steve Sandstrom** Client **Levi's Strauss & Co.**

(this page) Design Firm **Studio A. Inc.** Creative Director **Rachel Allgood** Art Directors **Jonathan McElroy** and **Rachel Allgood** Designers **Mary Swenson** and **Jonathan McElroy** Illustrator **Mary Swenson** Client **Ridgeview Inc. Hoisery** Fashion 110,111

(this page) Design Firm **Sibley/Peteet Design** Art Director and Designer **David Beck** Photographer **Sean McCormick** Client **Haggar Apparel Company** (opposite, from top) (**1**) Design Firm **Larsen Design & Interactive** Creative Director **Paul Wharton** Designer **Brad Serum** Client **Tulle & Dye** (**2**) Designer **Amy J. Nadaskay** Client **Little Giants Children's Clothing Store** (**3**) Design Firm **Lewis Advertising/Nashville** Art Director **Robert Froege** Client **Nellie's Originals** (**4**) Design Firm **Sayuri Studio** Art Director and Designer **Sayuri Shoji** Client **Issey Miyake Inc.** (**5**) Design Firm **Lewis Communications/Nashville** Art Director, Designer and Illustrator **Robert Froedge** Client **Snips & Snails Children's Clothing**

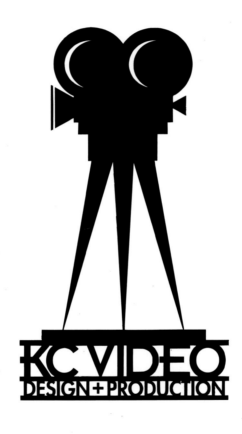

BRANDYE
JAMES

DIRECTOR

MR BIG FILM

Design Firm: **Felixsockwell.com** Designer and Illustrator **Felix Sockwell** Client: **Angelika Film Center**

MOXIE!
the santa monica film festival

ARTSY·FARTSY
PRODVCTIONS

K HL
PICTURES

PORTFOLIO

(this page) Design Firm **Envision** Creative Director, Art Director, Designer and Illustrator **Dara Schminke** Client **KingRam Funding (2)** Design Firm **Factor Design** Creative Director, Art Director, Designer **Isabel Braga** and **Rui Moura** Client **Portfolio Managers S.A.** (opposite, from top) (**1**) Design Firm **Brinkley Design** Creative Director **Leigh Brinkley** Creative Director **Tom Leifer** Art Director **Eva Ralle** Client **Booster** (**3**) Design Firm **Chris Herron Design** Creative Director, Art Director, Designer and Illustrator **Chris Herron** Client **New York Life Benefit Services LLC (4)** Design Firm **Chris Herron Design** Creative Director, Art Director, Designer **Bisturi** Art Directors **Isabel Braga** and **Rui Moura** Client **Portfolio Managers S.A.** Designer **Kit Cannon** Illustrator **Amy Faucette** Client **Charlotte Capital (5)** Design Firm **Savage Design Group, Inc.** Creative Director **Paula Savage** Art Director **Bo Bothe** Designers **Bo Bothe** and **Eric Hines** Client **Precision Investment Technologies**

BOOSTER

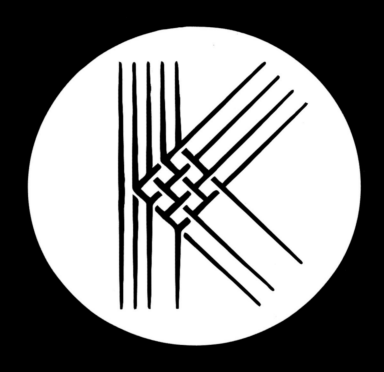

Design Firm **Judson Design** Art Director, Designer and Illustrator **Greg Valdez** Client **Kimberley Partners Inc.**

(this page) Design Firm **Gee & Chung Design** Creative Director, Art Director, Designer and Illustrator **Fani Chung** Client **Nanocosm Technologies, Inc.**

(from top) (**1 and opposite**) Design Firm **Becker Design** Creative Director, Art Director and Designer **Neil Becker** Client **CUNA Mutual Group** (**2**) Design Firm **AND** Art Director **Scott Arrowood** Client **Maxim First Security Bank** (**3**) Design Firm **Karlic Design Associates** Creative Director, Art Director and Designer **Ken Karlic** Client **Centre Solutions** (**4**) Design Firm **Coffe/Black Advertising** Creative Director **Troy Scillian** Art Director, Designer and Illustrator **Aaron Opsal** Client **State National Companies** (**5**) Design Firm **Michael Patrick Partners** Creative and Art Director **Darice Koziel** Designers **Connie Hwang** and **Ian Smith** Client Project Manager **Karen Milnes**

(from top) (1) Design Firm **David Carter Design Associates** Creative Director **Lori B. Wilson** Art Director **Sharon LeJeune** Designer and Illustrator **Tein Pham** Client **Sun International** (2) Design Firm **A/3** Creative and Art Director **Adrian Pulfer** Designers **Cliff Morgan** and **Adrian Pulfer** Client **Sundance** (3 and opposite) Design Firm **Chermayeff & Geismar Inc.** Client **Eli's Manhattan** (4) Design Firm **Summation** Creative Directors **Bart Welch** and **Tim Fisher** Illustrator **Bart Welch** Client **The Food Designers** (5) Design Firm **30/sixty design** Creative Director **Henry Vizcarra** Art Director **Chris Jaszkowiak** Designers **Gary Pelzman** and **Marilyn Pelzman** Client **King's Seafood Company**

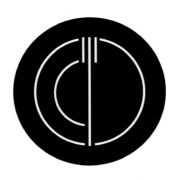

(from top) (**1**) Design Firm **Dula Image** Creative Director, Art Director and Designer **Michael Dula** Client **Creative Culinary Design** (**2**) Design Firm **SBG Partners** Art Director and Designer **Mark Bergman** Client **Monterey Pasta Co.** (**3**) Designer and Illustrator **Felix Sockwell** Client **Deep Sushi**

VERMONT
FLATBREAD CO.

(from top) (1) Design Firm **Judson Design** Creative Director **Mark Judson** Art Director and Designer **Jeff Davis** Illustrator **Morgan Bomar** Client **Office of the Mayor** (2) Design Firm **Iridium, a design agency** Creative Director and Designer **Jean Luc Denat** Client **Canadian Policy & Research Networks** (3) Design Firm **Graphic Content** Art Director and Designer **Art Garcia** Copywriter **Max Wright** Client **Texas Natural Resource Conservation Commission** (4) Design Firm **Greteman Group** Creative Director **Sonia Greteman** Art Directors **Sonia Greteman** and **James Strange** Designer **James Strange** Client **City of Wichita** (5) Design Firm **Kari Piippo Oy** Art Director and Designer **Kari Piippo** Client **City of Mikkeli**

Design Firm **Jill McCoy Design** Designer **Jill McCoy** Client **Santa Clara Valley Water District**

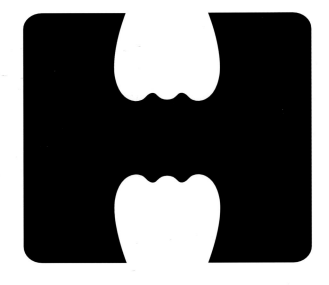

Design Firm **Sussner Design Company** Art Director **Derek Sussner** Designer **Ryan Carlson** Client **Life Time Fitness**

(from top) (**1**) Design Firm **Dennard Lacey & Associates** Creative Director and Art Director **Bob Dennard** Designer **Chris Wood** Client **VHA Voluntary Hospitals of America** (**2**) Design Firm **The Deborah Howard Agency Ltd.** Designer and Illustrator **Siri Nadler** Client **Planet Fitness Health Club** (**3**) Design Firm **Antista Fairclough** Creative Directors, Art Directors and Designers **Tom Antista** and **Thomas Fairclough** Client **Hospitality Procurement Services** (**4**) Design Firm **RBMM** Art Director, Designer and Illustrator **Tom Nynas** Client **Healthsteps** (**5**) Design Firm **Greteman Group** Creative Director **Sonia Greteman** Art Directors **Sonia Greteman** and **James Strange** Designer **Garrett Fresh** Client **Healing Horses Therapy**

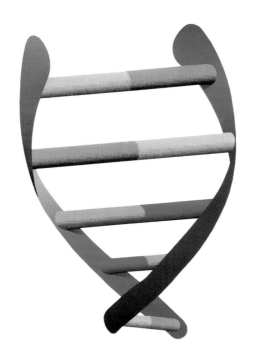

Design Firm **Gill Fishman Associates** Creative Director **Gill Fishman** Designer and Illustrator **Michael Persons** Client **Variagenics**

(from top) (1) Design Firm **Mirko Ilic Corp.** Art Director and Designer **Mirko Ilic** Client **The Time Hotel & Adam D. Tihany International** (2) Design Firm **Maddocks & Co.** Creative Director **Mary Scott** Designer **Amy Hirshman** Illustrator **Martin Elyard** Client **The Venetian** (3) Design Firm **RBMM** Art Director and Designer **Shayne Washburn** Client **Home Gate Studios & Suites** (4) Design Firm **Judson Design** Creative Director and Art Director **Mark Judson** Designers **Blake Miller** and **Jeff Davis** Illustrator **Andy Dearwater** Client **Hotel Galvez** (5) Design Firm **Squires & Co.** Creative Director, Art Director, Designer and Illustrator **Paul Black** Client **Hearth Side**

Design Firm **Greteman Group** Creative Director **Sonia Greteman** Art Directors and Designers **Sonia Greteman** and **James Strange** Client **Hotel at Old Town**

(from top) (1 & 3) Design Firm **Ogilvy & Mather** Creative Director **Brian Collins** Art Director and Designer **Brian Collins** Art Director and Designer **Felix Sockwell** Illustrators **Felix Sockwell** and **Tom Vasquez** Illustrator **Tom Vasquez** Client **Starwood** (2) Design Firm **Ogilvy & Mather** Art Director **Felix Sockwell** Designer **Felix Sockwell** Client **Starwood** Client **Starwood** (opposite) Design Firm **Ogilvy & Mather** Art Director **Brian Collins** Designer **Felix Sockwell** Client **Starwood**

Insurance, Landscaping 144,145

Design Firm **Felixsockwell.com** Art Director and Illustrator **Felix Sockwell** Client **Kaelson Landscaping**

(this page) Design Firm **Turner Duckworth** Creative Directors **David Turner** and **Bruce Duckworth** Designer **Anthony Biles** Client **Amazon.com** (opposite, from top) (**1**) Design Firm **Pentagram Design** Creative Director, Art Director and Designer **Kit Hinrichs** Client **Auto Web** (**2**) Design Firm **Stonedesign** Art Director and Designer **Geoffrey Stone** Client **Vidwan** (**3**) Design Firm **Media Ave.** Creative Director **Larry Laiken** Designer and Illustrator **Viktor Koen** Copywriters **Larry Laiken** and **Larry Snyder** Client **Media Ave.** (**4**) Design Firm **Signal Communications** Art Director and Designer **Scott Severson** Client **Promisemark** (**5**) Design Firm **Mires Design** Art Director **John Ball** Designer **Miguel Perez** Client **Ebay**

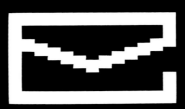

(from top) 1) Design Firm **Sibley/Peteet Design** Client **Sibley/Peteet Design (2)** Design Firm **Felixsockwell.com** Designer and Illustrator **Felix Sockwell** Client **Eself.com (3)** Design Firm **Pentagram Design** Art Director **Michael Bierut** Designers **Michael Bierut, Jacqueline Thaw** and **Brett Traylor (4)** Design Firm **Doublespace** Creative Director **Jane Kosstrin** Art Director and Designer **Jason Endres** Client: **Knowledge 2 Go (5)** Art Director, Creative Director and Designer **Les Kerr** Client **Geobility**

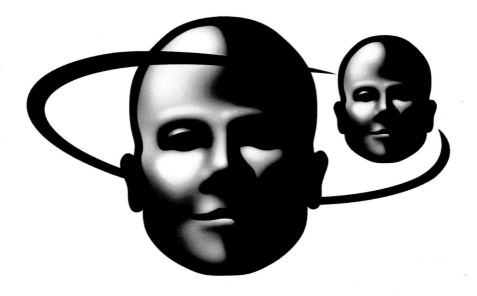

Design Firm **Hasan & Partners** Art Director **Kimmo Kivilanti** Designer and Illustrator **Jarkko Talonpoika** Client **Second Head** Internet **148,149**

WOODWORKS
Station

(from top) (1) Design Firm **Liska and Associates, Inc** Art Director **Steve Liska** Designer **Susan Carlson** Client **Heltzer Inc.** (2) Design Firm **Creative Soup Inc.** Creative Director, Designer and Illustrator **Mark Wilcox** Client **Beaulieu Commercial Carpet Manufacturing** (3) Design Firm **Overdrive (Design Ltd.)** Art Director **James Wilson** Designers **James Wilson** and **Matthew Labutte** Illustrator **Matthew Labutte** Client **Woodworks Station** (4) Design Firm **Nationsbanks Corp.** Client **Nationsbanks Corp.** Center Designers **Patrick Short** Designers **Patrick Short** Designers and **Brandon Scharr** Photographer and Illustrator **Brandon Scharr** Client **Drexel Heritage** (5) Design Firm **Pictogram Studio** Creative Directors **Stephanie Hooton** and **Hien Nguyen** Client **National Institute of Standards and Technology**

Design Firm **Hansen Design Company** Art Director and Designer **Pat Hansen** Client **The Loop Corporation**

Manufacturers **150,151**

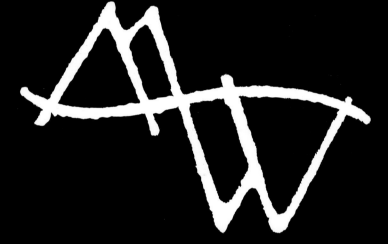

Design Firm **Planet Propaganda** Art Directors **Dana Lytle** and **Kevin Wade** Designers **Martha Graettinger** and **Kevin Wade** Client **Misty River Woodworks**

Manufacturers **152,153**

Design Firm **Benitez Design LLC** Creative Directors **Jack Herr** and **Chris Benitez** Client **Multimedia Live**

Multimedia **156,157**

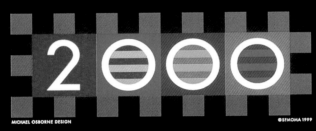

MICHAEL OSBORNE DESIGN ©SFMOMA 1999

SAN FRANCISCO MUSEUM OF MODERN ART

TheTech

(top) Design Firm **Chermayeff & Geismar Inc.** Client **Georgia O'Keeffe Museum** (bottom) Design Firm **Frankfurt Balkind Partners** Creative Director **Kent Hunter** Designer **Steven Fabrizio** Client **Tech Museum of Innovation**

CRAWFORD
MUSEUM
OF TRANSPORTATION AND INDUSTRY

(this page) Design Firm **Nesnadny & Schwartz** Creative and Art Director **Mark Schwartz** Designer **Greg Oznowich** Illustrator **Paul Rogers** Client **Crawford Museum of Transportation & Industry** (opposite, from top) (**1**) Creative Director and Designer **Steff Geissbuhler** Client **Toledo Museum of Art** (**2**) Design Firm **Woodpile Studios, Inc.** Creative and Art Director **George Jacoma** Designer and Illustrator **Peter Buttecali** Client **Jacoma Design** (**3**) Design Firm **Rick Johnson & Company** Creative Director **Ron Salzberg** Designer **Tim McGrath** Client **New Mexico Museum of Natural History** (**4**) Design Firm **Sullivan Perkins** Art Director and Designer **Myra J. Nowlin** Client **American Museum of Miniature Arts** (**5**) Design Firm **Rapp Collins Communcations** Art Director, Designer, Photographer and Illustrator **Yves Roux** Client **Minnetonka Center for the Arts**

(this spread) Design Firm **Landor Associates** Creative Director **Margaret Youngblood** Art Director and Designer **Doug Sellers** Client **The Exploratorium**

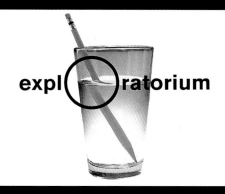

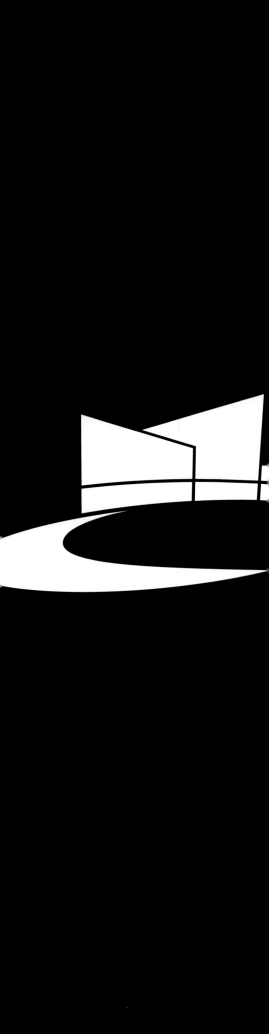

KineXUS

Design Firm **Peterson & Co.** Creative Director, Art Director, Designer and Illustrator **Nhan T. Pham** Client **Kinexus Museum of Moving Art**

(this page) Design Firm **Maverick Records** Art Directors and Designers **Kim Biggs** and **David Harlan** Client **Tantric** (opposite, from top) (**1**) Design Firm **Kari Piipo Oy** Art Director and Designer **Kari Piipo** Client **Mikkelin Musiikkiopisto** (**2**) Design Firm **Pennebaker.LMC** Art Director and Designer **Drew Ehrgott** Client **Last Eve** (**3**) Design Firm **Insight Design Communications** Art Directors **Sherrie Holdeman** and **Tracy Holdeman** Designer and Illustrator **Chris Parks** Client **Moko Music and Sound Design** (**4**) Design Firm **Automatic Art and Design** Art Director **Frank Gargulio** Designer **Charles Wilkin** Client **Capricorn Records** (**5**) Design Firm **Weissraum** Creative Director, Art Director and Designer **Bernd Brink** Client **Tiger**

Design Firm **Rickabaugh Graphics** Art Director **Eric Rickabaugh** Designers **Eric Rickabaugh** and **Dave Cap** Client **Jewel**

NEW LEAF

PAPER

Paper Companies 172,173

New Leaf Paper

Design Firm **Elixir Design Inc.** Creative Director **Jennifer Jerde** Designer and Photographer **Nathan Durrant** Client **New Leaf Paper**

(from top) (1) Design Firm **Joseph Rattan Design** Art Director and Designer **Joe Rattan** Illustrator **Iana McKnight** Client **Pasadena Paper Co.** (2) Design Firm **SBG Partners** Art Director and Designer **Mark Bergman** Client **Monterey Paper Co.** (3) Design Firm **Carmichael Lynch** Creative Director **Bill Thorburn** Designer **David Schrimpf** Client **Potlatch** (4) Design Firm **Keller & Company** Designer and Illustrator **Aaron Dietz** Client **Crane Paper** (5) Design Firm **Pedestrian** Creative Director, Art Director and Designer **Jason Endres** Client **Apeels (3M)**

(this page) Design Firm **Hawse Design Inc.** Creative Director **Robert Hawse** Designer and Illustrator **Matt Stevens** Client **Steve Knight Photography** (opposite, from top) (**1**) Design Firm **RBMM** Designer and Illustrator **Dan Birlew** Client **Triclops** Client **Starkwhite** Client **Dave Shafer Photography** (**3**) Design Firm **Automatic Art and Design** Art Director and Designer **Charles Wilkin** Client **Piere D'Amico Photography** (**4**) Design Firm **Sibley/Peteet Design** Client **Chris Christensen** (**5**) Design Firm **Thinking Caps** Creative Director and Designer **Julie Henson** Client **Spicer Photogaphy**

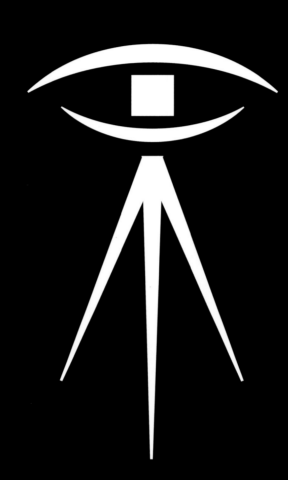

(this page) Design Firm **David Clark Design** Designer **David Clark** Client **Cole/Smallwood Photographers** (opposite, from top) (**1**) Design Firm **White Plus** Art Director **Trino Nuovo** Designer **Victoria Barry** Photographer **Will Nelson** Client **Debmar Studios** (**2**) Design Firm **Duffy Design** Art Director, Designer and Illustrator **Neil Powell** Client **Mark Weiss Photography** (**3**) Design Firm **Greteman Group** Creative and Art Director **Sonia Greteman** Designer **James Strange** Client **Golfoto** (**4**) Design Firm **Signal Communications** Art Director and Designer **Scott Severson** Client **Wagman & Wagman** (**5**) Design Firm **Wink** Art Directors **Scott Thares** and **Richard Boynton** Designer and Illustrator **Scott Thares** Client **Setterholm Productions**

(this page, from top) (1) Design Firm **AND** Creative Directors and Designers **Scott Arrowood** and **Douglas Dearden** Client **Impact (2)** Design Firm **Savage Design Group Inc.** Creative Director **Paula Savage** Art Director **Doug Hebert** and **Alyssum Klopp** Client **Western Lithograph (3)** Design Firm **Qualcomm Design Group** Creative Director **Christopher Lee** Designers **Christopher Lee** and **Adam Rowe** Client **Rush Press (4)** Design Firm **Eisenberg and Associates** Creative Director **Saul Torres** Art Director, Designer and Illustrator **Dona Mitcham** Client **McCord Printing (5)** Design Firm **Larsen Design Office Inc.** Art Directors **Tim Larsen** and **Richelle Huff** Designer **Sascha Boecker** Client **Brown Printing** (opposite page) Design Firm **Toth Advertising** Creative Director **Mike Toth** Art Director **Margo Chase** Designers **Margo Chase** and **Jonathan Sample** Client **Toth Advertising**

FLAMERITE
LIGHTERS

OLOGI™

COQUÍCO

(from top) **(1 & 2)** Design Firm **Charles S. Anderson Design** Art Director **Todd Piper-Hauswirth** Designers **Todd Piper-Hauswirth** and **Kyle Hames** Client **Flamerite (3 and opposite)** Design Firm **Turner Duckworth** Creative Directors **David Turner** and **Bruce Duckworth** Designer **David Turner** Client **Ologi (4)** Design Firm **Supon Design Group** Creative Director **Supon Phornibrunlit** Art Directors **Supon Phornibrunlit** and **Lillie Fujinaga** Designer **Pum Mek-Aroonreung** Client **Coquico (5)** Design Firm **Rassman Design** Art Director **John Rassman** Designer **Lyn D'Amato** Copywriter **Bruce Abels** Client **Ocean Journey**

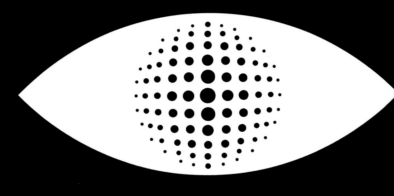

(this page) Design Firm **Kellum McClain Inc.** Creative Director **John Athorn** Designer **Ron Kellum** Client **Sensormatic Anti-Theft Technology** (opposite, from top) (**1**) Design Firm **Mires Design** Art Director **Scott Mires** Designer **Miguel Perez** Client **Cartronics Shopping Cart Loss Prevention** (**2**) Design Firm **AND** Creative Director and Designer **Douglas Dearden** Client **Wristgliders** (**3**) Design Firm **SBG Partners** Art Director **Mark Bergman** Designer **Jessie McAnulty** Illustrator **Philip Yip** Client **Borden, Inc.** (**4**) Design Firm **Graphic Design Society** Creative Director and Designer **Tim A. Frame** Client **Pressure Connections Pressure Sensitive Fittings** (**5**) Design Firm **Keith Harris Design** Creative and Art Director **Keith Harris** Client **Re-Originals Down Under Spare-Parts Supplier**

TETHER CAM

TETHER CAM

TETHER CAM

TETHER CAM

TETHER CAM

(this page) Design Firm **Iridium, a design agency** Creative Director Jean-Luc Denat Art Director **Mario L'Écuyer** Designers **Mario L'Écuyer** and Etienne Bessette Client **Tether Cam Systems Inc. Aerial Camera Platform**

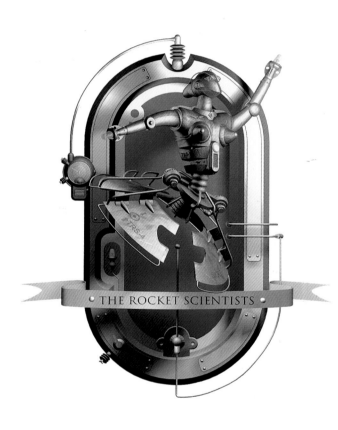

THE ROCKET SCIENTISTS

Professional Services 188,189

Design Firm **The Rocket Scientists** Creative Director **Charl Ritter** Art Director, Designer and Illustrator **Eduard Claassen** Client **The Rocket Scientists**

gettuit.com

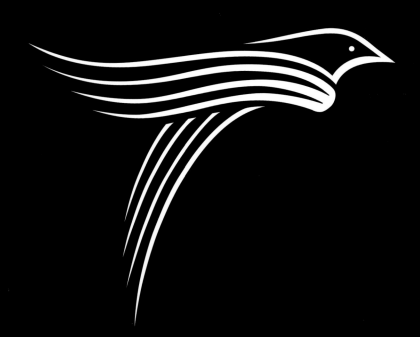

Design Firm **Muller & Company** Art Director **John Muller** Designer **Dave Swearingen** Client **Tazewell**

FRINGE HAIR STUDIO

(from top) (1) Design Firm **Matthias Schafer Design** Creative Director, Art Director, Designer and Illustrator **Matthias Schafer** Client **PR—Team of the Fachhochschule Wiesbaden (2)** Design Firm **Exem Company** Designer **Jeff Culver** Client **Exem Software Company (3)** Design Firm **Keith Harris Design** Creative Director, Art Director and Designer **Keith Harris** Client **Antik und Auktionshaus Adamski (4)** Design Firm **Insight Design Communications** Art Directors, Designers and Illustrators **Sherrie Holdeman** and **Tracy Holdeman** Client **Cooper Waste Management System (5)** Design Firm **Isocurve, formerly Studio A Inc.** Creative Director **Rachel Allgood** and **Rachel Allgood** Art Directors **Jonathan McElroy** and **Rachel Allgood** Designer **Jonathan McElroy** Client **Meisner Acrylic Casting Llc**

Design Firm **Keith Harris Design** Creative Director, Art Director and Designer **Keith Harris** Client Antik und Auktionshaus Adamski (Adamski Aucion and Antiques)

Design Firm **Parachute** Art Director and Designer **Bob Upton** Photographer **Paul Irmiter** Client **Parachute**

(from top) **(1)** Design Firm **Myra Nowlin** Art Director and Designer **Myra J. Nowlin** Client **Wiley Publishing Co. (2)** Design Firm **Kirima Design Office** Art Director and Designer **Harumi Kirima** Client **Kohrinsha-Syuppan (3)** Design Firm **RBMM** Creative Director **Brian Boyd** Designer **Rolando Murillo** Client **Putnam Books (4)** Design Firm **Dennard Lacey & Associates** Creative Director, Art Director, Designer and Illustrator **Bob Dennard** Client **Dallas Business Committee for the Arts Newsletter (5)** Design Firm **Gillespie Designs** Art Director **Tom McManimon** Designers **Tom McManimon** and **Judy Mazziotti** Client **Recording for the Blind & Dyslexic**

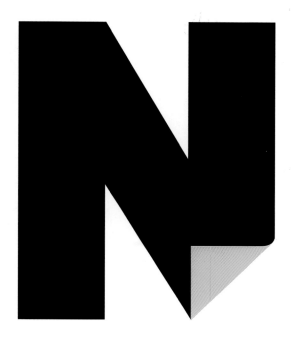

Design Firm **A/3** Creative Director, Art Director and Designer **Adrian Pulfer** Client **Nextpage Corporation (publishing software manufacturer)** Publishing **198,199**

(this spread) Design Firm **Hornall Anderson Design Works** Art Director **Jack Anderson** Designers **Jack Anderson, Mary Hermes, Gretchen Cook, Andrew Smith, Julie Lock, Holly Craven, Elmer Dela Cruz, Belinda Bowling** and **Amy Fawcette** Brand/Naming Consultant **Tyler Cartier** Illustrators **Gretchen Cook** and **Andrew Smith** Client **Space Needle**

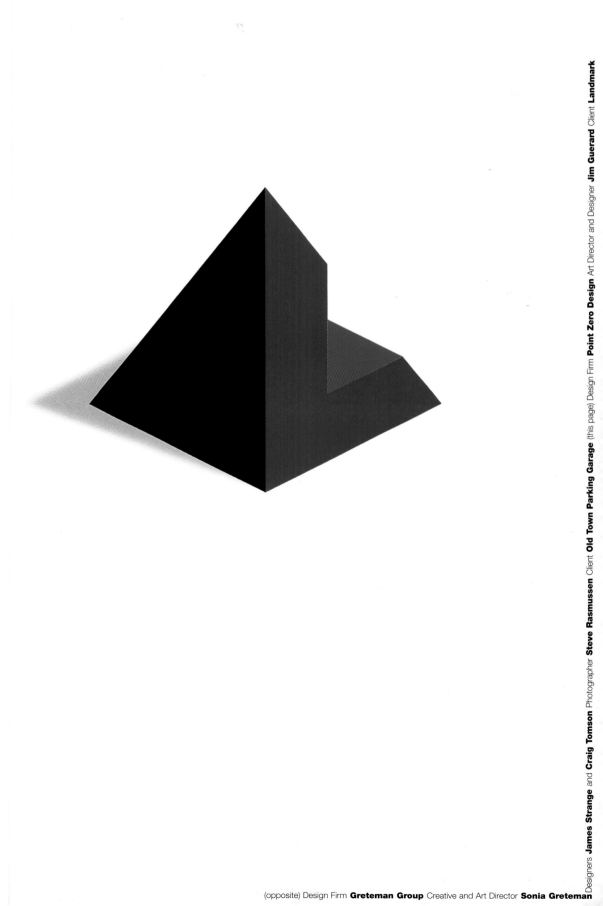

Designers **James Strange** and **Craig Tomson** Photographer **Steve Rasmussen** Client **Old Town Parking Garage** (this page) Design Firm **Point Zero Design** Art Director and Designer **Jim Guerard** Client **Landmark**

(opposite) Design Firm **Greteman Group** Creative and Art Director **Sonia Greteman**

L I N D B E R G H

CITY CENTER

(from top) (1) Design Firm **ZGraphics Ltd.** Art Director **Lou Ann Zeller** Designer **Gregg Rojewski** Client **Dundee Main Street Downtown Revitalization Campaign (2)** Design Firm **RBMM** Art Director, Designer and Illustrator **Tom Nynas** Client **Storage Solutions (3)** Design Firm **Overdrive (Design Ltd.)** Art Director, Designer and Illustrator **James Wilson** Client **Smith Properties (4)** Design Firm **Creadesign Corp.** Creative Director and Designer **Ebru Pinar** Client **Eagle Vision Realty Corp. (5)** Design Firm **Vanderbyl Design** Creative Director, Art Director and Designer **Michael Vanderbyl** Client **The Castle Group (real estate development)**

E

Design Firm **Essex Two** Creative Directors **Joseph Michael Essex** and **Nancy Denney Essex** Art Director and Designer **Joseph Michael Essex** Client **Equity Residential Properties** Real Estate 206,207

(this page) Design Firm **Rick Johnson & Company** Creative Director **Ron Salzberg** Designer **Tim McGrath** Client **Santa Ana Golf Club** (opposite, from top) (**1, 2, 4 & 5**) Design Firm **M Group** with **Sibley Peteet Design** Art Director **Tim McClure** Creative Director **Tim Brinkman** Creative Director **Mark Brinkman** Designer **Mark Brinkman** Illustrators **Mark Brinkman** and **Rex Peteet** Client **Barton Creek Country Club** (**3**) Design Firm **Sherry Matthews Advertising** with **Sibley Peteet Design** Art Director, Designer and Illustrator **Mark Brinkman** Client **Comanche Trace Ranch**

Design Firm **Judson Design** Art Directors **Mark Judson** and **Jeff Davis** Creative Director **Mark Judson** Designer and Illustrator **Jeff Davis** Client **Luigi's Restaurant**

BLACK'S
BAR AND KITCHEN

(this page) Design Firm **Dennard Lacey & Associates** Art Direcotor, Creative Director and Designer **Bob Dennard** Illustrator **James Lacey** Client **Steak & Ale Restaurant** (opposite, from top) (**1**) Design Firm **Automatic Art and Design** Art Director and Designer **Charles Wilkin** Client **Planet Coffee** (**2**) Design Firm **Compass Design** Designer **Mitch Lindgren** Client **Sunrise Bakery** (**3**) Design Firm **Graphic Design Society** Creative Directors **Tim A. Frame** and **Maribeth Gatchauan** Designer **Tim A. Frame** Client **Haiku (Asian restaurant)** (**4**) Design Firm **Judson Design** Creative Director **Mark Judson** Art Director, Designer and Illustrator **Greg Valdez** Client **Hunt Room (English-style restaurant at the Warwick Hotel)** (**5**) Design Firm **Prejean LoBue** Art Directors **Gary LoBue, Jr.** and **Ashley Mattocks** Creative Director **Lori B. Wilson** Designer and Illustrator **Gary LoBue, Jr.** Client **David Carter Graphic Design Associates (for hotel/restaurants)**

PLANET COFFEE
AND TEA COMPANY

SUNRISE GOURMET™

SuLAN'S

BAYSIDE

BUFFET

(this page) Design Firm **Craig Frazier Studio** Art Director, Designer and Illustrator **Craig Frazier** Client **Sushi Ran** (opposite, from top) (**1**) Design Firm **Pentagram Design** Art Director **Paula Scher** Designers **Paula Scher** and **Anke Stohlam** Client **Buddakan** (**2**) Designer **Amy J. Nadaskay** Illustrator **Eric Larson** Client **Insignia** (**2**) Design Firm **Kosaka Design** Creative Director **Wayne Kosaka** Designer **Jeff Welch** Client **Kimpton Group/Atwood Cafe** (**4**) Design Firm **Duffy Minneapolis** Creative Director **Joe Duffy** Art Director, Designer and Illustrator **Alan Colvin** Client: **Nordstrom Coffee House** (**5**) Design Firm **Signal Communications** Art Director and Designer **Scott Severson** Client **Butterfield 9 Restaurant**

S U S H I

R A N

BUDDAKAN

BUDDAKAN

(this page) Design Firm **Dula Image Group** Creative Director, Art Director, Designer and Illustrator: **Michael Dula** Client **Aloha Restaurants, Inc.** (opposite, from top) (**1**) Design Firm **Total Creative** Art Director **Rod Dyer** Designer and Illustrator **Michael Doret** Client **Hollywood & Vive Diner** (**2**) Design Firm **Duffy Design** Creative Director **Joe Duffy** Art Director, Designer and Illustrator **Alan Colvin** Client **La Madeleine** (**3**) Design Firm **Margo Chase Design** Designer **Brian Hunt** Client **Hard Rock Hotel & Casino** (**4**) Design Firm **Menefee and Partners /Insight Design Communications** Creative Director **Greg Menefee** Art Directors, Designers and Illustrators **Sherrie Holdeman** and **Tracy Holdeman** Project Coordinator **Chris Anderson** Client **Carlos O'Kelly's Mexican Cafe** (**5**) Design Firm **Sayles Graphic Design** Creative Director, Art Director, Designer and Illustrator **John Sayles** Client **Messodi's**

O C E A N P L A C E

Design Firm **Sabingrafik, Inc.** Art Director **Marilee Bankert** Illustrator **Tracy Sabin** Client **Oceanplace Shopping Center**

Design Firm **Summa Communications** Creative Director **Josep Maria Mir** Art Director **Wladimir Marnich** Designers **Wladimir Marnich** and **Anna Sodupe** Illustrator **Anna Sodupe** Client: **Miquel Alimentació (supermarket chain)** 222,223

(this page) Design Firm **Joseph Rattan Design** Art Director, Designer and Illustrator **Diana McKnight** Client **Prime Retail (retail outlet builder/manager)**

Design Firm **Antista Fairclough** Creative and Art Directors **Tom Antista** and **Thomas Fairclough** Designer **Tom Antista** Illustrator **Kevin Newman** Client **Clark Refining & Marketing** Retail **224,225**

CENTRAL YAMAHA

(from top) (1) Design Firm **Focus 2** Art Director **Todd Hart** Designer **Duane King** Client **ID Software** (2) Design Firm **Joseph Rattan Design** Art Director and Designer **Brandon Murphy** Illustrators **Brandon Murphy** and **Diana McKnight** Client **Rainforest Shopping Center** (3) Design Firm **Engage Advertising** Creative Director **Roman Milo** Art Director and Designer **Tomasz Borowicz** Illustrator **Daria Widlak** Copywriter **Bruce Hiebert** Client **HDS** (4) Design Firm **Banowetz & Company** Creative Director **Leon Banowetz** Designer **Kris Murphy** Client **Central Yamaha** (5) Design Firm **Sommese Design** Art Director, Designer and Illustrator **Lanny Sommese** Client **Aquatics 'n Exotics Pet Shops** (opposite page) Design Firm **Sommese Design** Art Director and Illustrator **Kristin Sommese** Photographers **Kristin Sommese** and **Dick Ackley** Client **Medusa's Clothing**

THE
OLD
KIRK

(this page) Design Firm **Pentagram Design** Art Director **Justus Oehler** Client **The Old Kirk** (opposite, from top) (**1**) Design Firm **Principia Graphica** Art Director **Heidi Rickabaugh** Designer **Clint Gorthy** Client **Oregon Corporation for Affordable Housing** (**2**) Design Firm **Greenhaus** Art Director **Craig Fuller** Illustrator **Tracy Sabin** Client **San Diego Zoo** (**3**) Design Firm **Graphic Content Inc.** Art Director and Designer **Art Garcia** Client **Mothers Against Drunk Driving** (**4**) Design Firm **Pentagram Design** Art Director **Michael Gericke** Client **Women's Venture Fund** (**5**) Design Firm **RBMM** Art Director, Designer and Illustrator **Tom Nynas** Client **Heaven Connection**

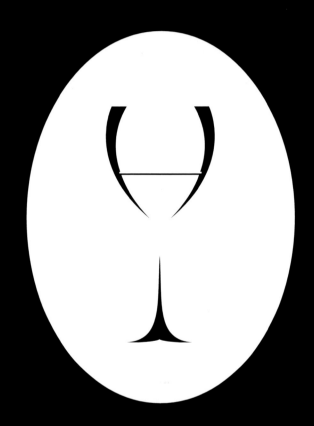

Design Firm **RBMM** Art Director, Designer and Illustrator **Tom Nynas** Client **Domaine Haleaux**

Design Firm **Sandstrom Design** Creative and Art Director **Steve Sandstrom** Production Designer **Starlee Matz** Project Manager **Kathy Middleton** Client **Miller**

(from top) (1) Design Firm **Watts Design** Designer and Illustrator **Peter Watts** Client **Beechwood Winery (2)** Design Firm **Silk Pearce** Creative Director **Peter Silk** Designer **James Phelan** Illustrator **Ron Mercer** Client **Piercefield Estate (3)** Design Firm **Sandstrom Design** Creative Director **Steve Sandstrom** Client **Blue Heron (4)** Design Firm **Michael Schwab Studio** Art Director **Mark Dolin** Designer and Illustrator **Michael Schwab** Client **Robert Mondavi (5)** Design Firm **Judson Design** Creative Director **Mark Judson** Art Director, Designer and Illustrator **Jeff Davis** Client **Water Street Brewing Company**

Design Firm **Sandstrom Design** Creative Director **Steve Sandstrom**

(from top) (1) Design Firm **Mires Design** Art Director and Designer **José A. Serrano** Client **Chaos Lures** (2) Design Firm **Mires Design** Creative and Art Director **John Ball** Designer **Deborah Hom** Client **Nike** (3) Design Firm **Sibley Peteet Design** Creative Director **Matt Heck** Art Director and Designer **Mark Brinkman** Client **Hyde Park Gym** (4) Design Firm **AND** Creative Directors and Designers **Scott Arrowood** and **Douglas Dearden** Client **Yellow Jackets** (5) Design Firm **Mires Design** Creative and Art Director **José A. Serrano** Designer **Miguel Perez** Client: **San Diego Chargers**

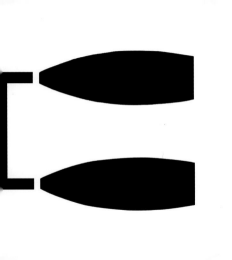

Clients

Design Firms

PhotographersIllustrators

DesignersCreativeDirectorsArtDirectors

Index

doug baldwin

writer

TRAVELON

(from top) (1) Design Firm **BEK** Creative Director, Art Director and Designer **Bülent Erkman** Client **Türsab (2)** Design Firm **Murat Bodur Design** Designer **Murat Bodur Design** Designer **Murat Bodur** Client **Travelon (3)** Design Firm **Red Herring Design** Creative Director **Carol Bobolts** Designer **Matthew Bouloutian** Client **History Channel International (4)** Design Firm **Hixo, Inc.** Art Director **Mike Hicks** Designer **Matt Heck** Client **Travel Fest (5)** Design Firm **Prejean LoBue** Creative Director, Art Director, Designer and Illustrator **Gary LoBue, Jr.** Client **Aegean Tours, LLP**

Design Firm **Duffy Minneapolis** Creative Director **Joe Duffy** Art Director and Illustrator **Tom Riddle** Designers **Tom Riddle** and **Nate Hinz** Copywriter **John Jarvis** Client **International Transportation Corp.**

Design Firm **Greteman Group** Creative Director **Sonia Greteman** Art Director and Designer **James Strange** Client **Executive Aircraft**

(this page) Design Firm **Amster Yard** Creative Director **Jeff Weiss** Art Directors **Casey Grady** and **Ty Baker** Designers **Benjamin Bailey, Ricardo Lopes, Dennis Balk** and **Raymond Byron** Clients **Various Soccer Teams**